EXCITING
india

a visual journey

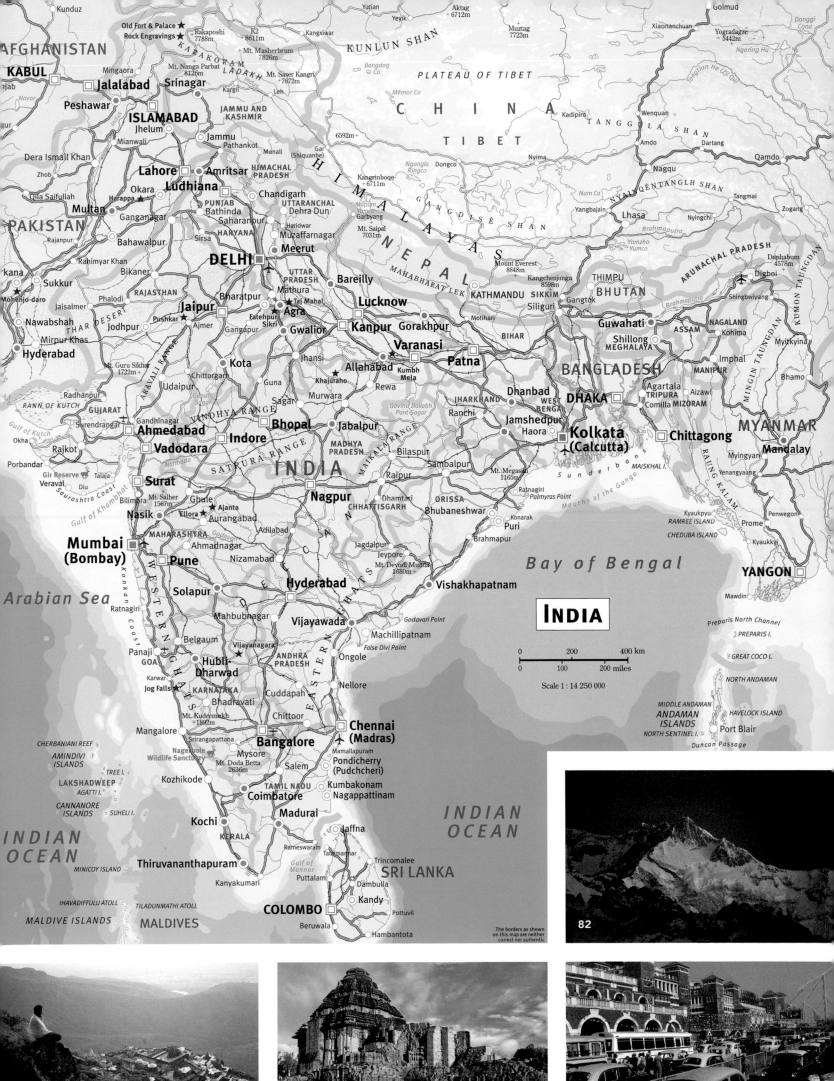

INDIA

AFGHANISTAN

KABUL
Jalalabad
Peshawar
ISLAMABAD

Old Fort & Palace ★
Rock Engravings ★

Mingaora
Rakaposhi 7788m
K2 8611m
Kangxiwar

KUNLUN SHAN

Yeyik
Yutian

Aktag 6712m

Muztag 7723m

Xiaonanchuan

Golmud
Yograidagze 5442m
Ngoring Hu

Donggi Cona

PLATEAU OF TIBET

KARAKORAM
Mt. Masherbrum 7826m
Mt. Nanga Parbat 8126m
Mt. Saser Kangri 7672m

LADAKH
Kargil
Leh

Bangdog Co

C H I N A

TIBET

Mêmar Co

6592m

Kadipiro
T A N G G U L A   S H A N

Wenquan

Nagqu

Tangmai
Zogang

Srinagar
Jammu
JAMMU AND KASHMIR

Pathankot
Manali
Gar (Shiquanhe)

Nyima

Lhasa
Nyingchi

Qamdo

Jhelum
Mianwali

Dera Ismail Khan

Lahore
Amritsar
Ludhiana

Okara
Harappa ★
HIMACHAL PRADESH

PUNJAB
Chandigarh
UTTARANCHAL
Dehra Dun

Kangrinboqe 6711m
Ngangla Ringco

Dongco

Mapam Yumco
Garbyang
Mt. Saipal 7031m

Yangbajain
NYAINQÊNTANGLH SHAN

Yamzho Yumco

Brahmaputra

ARUNACHAL PRADESH

Daphabum 4578m
Digboi

Multan
Qila Saifullah
Zhob

PAKISTAN

Bathinda
Saharanpur
Haridwar
Muzaffarnagar

Ganganagar
HARYANA
Sirsa

Rajanpur

Bahawalpur

Bikaner

Meerut

DELHI

UTTAR PRADESH

Bareilly

NEPAL

MAHABHARAT LEK

Mount Everest 8848m

Kangchenjunga 8598m

THIMPU
BHUTAN

Shingbwiyang

KUMON TAUNGDAN

MINGIN TAUNGDAN

Rahimyar Khan

Sukkur

Nawabshah

Mohenjo-daro ★

Hyderabad

Mirpur Khas

Jaisalmer

RAJASTHAN

Jaipur

Jodhpur
Pushkar ★
Ajmer

Bharatpur
Mathura
Fatehpur Sikri
Agra
Taj Mahal

Gwalior

Lucknow
Kanpur
Gorakhpur

Varanasi
Allahabad
Kumbh Mela

KATHMANDU
Motihari
BIHAR

Patna

SIKKIM
Siliguri
Gangtok

Guwahati
Shillong
MEGHALAYA

NAGALAND
Kohima

ASSAM

Imphal
MANIPUR

Myitkyina

Bhamo

THAR DESERT

Radhanpur

ARAVALI RANGE

Mt. Guru Sikhar 1722m

Kota
Chittorgarh
Udaipur

Guna

Jhansi
Khajuraho
Rewa

Sagar
Murwara

JHARKHAND
Ranchi

Dhanbad

WEST BENGAL

DHAKA
Agartala
TRIPURA
Comilla
MIZORAM

Aizawl

MYANMAR

RANN OF KUTCH

GUJARAT

Surendranagar
Gandhinagar

Ahmedabad
Vadodara
Indore

Bhopal

VINDHYA RANGE

MADHYA PRADESH

Jabalpur

SATPURA RANGE

Bilaspur

MAIKALA RANGE

Raipur

Govind Ballabh Pant Sagar

Jamshedpur
Haora
Kolkata (Calcutta)

Chittagong

Mandalay

Myingyan

Gulf of Kutch
Okha

Rajkot
Porbandar

Gir Reserve
Veraval
Talaja
Diu

Saurashtra Coast

Bilimora
Ghule
Mt. Salher 1567m

Surat

Nasik
Ellora ★
Ajanta ★
Aurangabad

INDIA

Narmada

Nagpur

Dhamtari

CHHATTISGARH

Sambalpur

Mt. Megasini 1165m

Sunderbans
MAISKHAL I.

RAUNG KALAM

Yenangyaung
Venangyaung

Prome

Kyaukpyu
RAMREE ISLAND

CHEDUBA ISLAND

Penwegon

Kyaukkyi

Gulf of Khambhat

DECCAN

Mumbai (Bombay)

Pune

Solapur

Ahmadnagar

Adilabad

Nizamabad

Jagdalpur
Mt. Devodi Munda 1680m

ORISSA

Bhubaneshwar

Puri
Konarak

Brahmapur
Ratnagiri
Palmyras Point

Mouths of the Ganga

Bay of Bengal

YANGON

Mawdin

KONKAN COAST

Ratnagiri

WESTERN GHATS

Mahbubnagar

Hyderabad

Vijayawada

Vishakhapatnam

Godavari Point

Preparis North Channel

PREPARIS I.

Arabian Sea

Belgaum

Panaji
GOA
Karwar

Hubli-Dharwad

Jog Falls

Vijayanagara ★

ANDHRA PRADESH

Ongole

Machillipatnam
False Divi Point

GREAT COCO I.

NORTH ANDAMAN

Scale 1 : 14 250 000

0   200   400 km
0   100   200 miles

Bhadravati
Mt. Kudremukh 1892m

Cuddapah

Nellore

MIDDLE ANDAMAN

ANDAMAN ISLANDS

HAVELOCK ISLAND

NORTH SENTINEL I.
Port Blair
Duncan Passage

CHERBANIANI REEF

AMINDIVI ISLANDS

TREE I.

LAKSHADWEEP
AGATTI I.

CANNANORE ISLANDS
SUHELI I.

Mangalore

Chittoor

EASTERN GHATS

Srirangapattana
Bangalore

Mysore
Mt. Doda Betta 2636m

Nagerhole Wildlife Sanctuary

Salem

Chennai (Madras)

Pondicherry (Pudchcheri)

Mamallapuram

INDIAN OCEAN

INDIAN OCEAN

Kozhikode

KERALA

Kochi

Thiruvananthapuram

MINICOY ISLAND

KARNATAKA

Coimbatore
TAMIL NADU
Kumbakonam
Nagappattinam

Madurai

Jaffna

Rameswaram
Talaimannar

Trincomalee

Kanyakumari

Gulf of Mannar

SRI LANKA
Puttalam

Dambulla

Kandy

IHAVADIFFULU ATOLL
TILADUNMATHI ATOLL

MALDIVE ISLANDS

MALDIVES

COLOMBO
Pottuvil

Beruwala

Hambantota

The borders as shown on this map are neither correct nor authentic.

72

76

78

82

namaste!

India is one of the most richly rewarding regions of the world to visit. Her scenery is varied and exciting, her history and culture are lived experiences, and the openness and friendliness of her people are legendary.

DERIVING HER NAME from the river Indus, India is a country of subcontinental dimensions. The home of one of the earliest civilizations on earth and several of the world's great religions, India's historical and cultural heritage dates back several centuries. She has changed and reshaped herself through the ages, forever producing new forms of cultures and absorbing new influences. India is, besides, a country of amazing contrasts and diversity, with a physical environment that ranges from thickly populated plains, awe-inspiring mountains and palm-fringed golden beaches, to dense rainforests. India boasts a wonderful mix of tradition and modernity that finds its best expression in the distinctive lifestyles of the people who live across this vast land. The people of India are also her greatest wealth, borne out by the fact that India is the world's largest secular democracy, and home to over 1,000 million people.

Top: A traditional South Indian girl holding a *thali* (plate) of *diyas* (lamps) – the traditional Indian form of welcome.
Facing page: The majestic Sivasamudram Falls in Karnataka – a telling reminder of nature's bounty.

welcome to majestic india!

Clockwise from top left:
Terraced cultivation in the lower reaches of the Himalayas. Dancers rehearsing at Kalakshetra, an academy of classical dance in Chennai. A view of the desert city of Jaisalmer in Rajasthan – the ramparts of Jaisalmer fort can be seen in the background. A streetside shopkeeper displays his wares – bales of colourful wool.

ARK TWAIN'S DESCRIPTION more than a century ago – "the land of dreams and contrasts, of palaces and hovels . . . of giants and Aladdin lamps, of tigers and elephants, of cobras and the jungle, the country of a hundred nations, of a thousand religions and a million gods," – encapsulates the wondrous variety and bewildering contradictions that are still true of India today. Bustling cities alongside dusty villages where elders sit in council under the shade of the banyan, slums that hover at the fringes of high-rises, camels and cows and wild-haired *sadhus* – these are but some of the elements that make India a fascinating travel destination.

Far left: Men sitting around campfires at India's largest cattle fair, in Pushkar, Rajasthan.
Left: A *sadhu* in ashes meditating at the banks of the Ganges at Benares.
Below: A solitary boatman on the Ganges.

a rich historical record

Successive waves of settlers – sometimes bringing goods for trade, sometimes armies to conquer territory, and sometimes in search of land and peace – have left an indelible mark on the landscape and cultures of India.

THE EARLIEST KNOWN INDIAN CIVILIZATION is that of the Indus Valley (*c.* 3rd millennium BC) centred on Harappa and Mohenjodaro, now in Pakistan. The Aryans from Central Asia were the first invaders: they spread through north India to Bengal, displacing the Dravidian inhabitants. The Aryan religion based on the *Vedas* was incorporated into Brahminism or early Hinduism. Alexander the Great invaded the Punjab in 327 BC, but the Greeks were driven out by Chandragupta of the Mauryan empire. Hinduism was the state religion until the reign of King Ashoka, who replaced it with Buddhism.

On Ashoka's death, the Mauryan empire disintegrated and northern India was then governed by a succession of dynasties until it succumbed to the

Facing page, clockwise from top left: Terracotta cart, Harappan civilization, *c.* 2700 BC.
Sculpture depicting the Didarganj *yakshi*.
Painting showing the *tantric* deity Tara, late 19th century.
This page, clockwise from far left: Stone Buddha head, Sarnath, 5th century.
An ancient Hindu seal.
Unicorn seal, Harappan civilization, *c.* 2700 BC.
The ramparts of an ancient fort.

Turks and Persians under Mahmud of Ghazni. These separate Muslim kingdoms were in turn subdued by Babur (1526), the founder of the Mughal empire. During the reign of Akbar (1556–1605), Mughal power was extended to most of northern and central India. Mughal architecture reached its peak under the rule of Shah Jahan (1627–58), but the empire disintegrated after the reign of Aurangzeb (1658–1707).

European interest in India began with Vasco da Gama's arrival (1498) at Calicut. During the 1600s, the British East India Company established trading posts at Surat, Bombay and Calcutta, driving off Portuguese and Dutch opposition. With the rapid decline of the Mughals, the British and the French extended their influence over the native states in the 18th century. This gave rise to Anglo-French conflict, which culminated in the expulsion of the French by the military victories of Clive. By 1850, the British Raj covered the whole of India.

Above: Sword of Tipu Sultan, Srirangapatnam, AD 1795.
Below: Detail of marble inlay work on the sandstone gateway of Akbar's tomb at Sikandra, Agra.

Far left: Gold coin of Mughal emperor Shahjahan.
Left: Illustrated folio of the *Baburnama*, depicting a royal hunt. The manuscript chronicles the life and times of the first Mughal emperor, Babur.
Below: The still waters of a river reflect the fort built on its bank.

Right: Early missionaries from Portugal came by sea to Goa on the western coast of India.
Below: A view of the Rashtrapati Bhavan in New Delhi, built in Indo-Saracenic style by Corbusier and Baker.

THE INDIAN DESIRE for self-government led to the formation of the Indian National Congress (1885), and after the First World War, Mahatma Gandhi led a national movement of passive resistance against British rule that finally brought independence to India. Soon thereafter, on August 17, 1947, the subcontinent was partitioned between India and Pakistan.

Far left: A decorative element of the Victoria Memorial in Calcutta, conceived by Lord Curzon as a monument to Queen Victoria.
Below: 'Court House Street', Calcutta, a painting by James Baillie Fraser.
Bottom: The camel-borne Border Security Force of India at Beating Retreat, a ceremony that celebrates the significance of the armed forces in the Republic of India.

a nation of dazzling ethnic diversity

The diversity among India's billion-strong citizens is mind-boggling, and the numerous ethnic and cultural variations make for an incredible array of humanity.

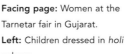

Facing page: Women at the Tarnetar fair in Gujarat.
Left: Children dressed in *holi* colours.
Middle left: Bismillah Khan – India's renowned *shehnai* player.
Middle right: A Sikh Nihang warrior.
Bottom: A young woman in traditional dress and jewellery.

INDIA IS A LAND of over a billion people but it is impossible to characterize a typical Indian, given the immense diversity of its peoples. Centuries of conquests and colonization, and constant interaction with traders, missionaries and settlers, have given rise to many broad ethnic and cultural groups in today's India. The Adivasi is the archetypal Indian who inhabits the mountains and forests. The dark-skinned Dravidians live in the fertile plains of the south. The Aryans of the north came to India from Central Asia, while Arabs, Parsis and Bahais came from the Middle East and settled along the western coast. Indians are also divided along religious and caste lines, with the Hindus predominating as a religious group.

THE HINDUS are divided according to caste, a four-tiered system that predetermines the profession and status of individuals. At the top of the caste hierarchy are the Brahmins, who are intellectuals or priests. Then come the Kshatriyas, or warriors, followed by the Vaishyas – businessmen or traders. The Shudras are on the bottom rung of the ladder, doing menial jobs. Outside the divisions of caste are the outcastes – the lowest of the low.

Below left: An aged goatherd from rural India.
Below right: The driver of a steam locomotive – India boasts the largest railway network in the world.
Bottom: Muslim children at a traditional Islamic school, or *madrasa*.

Facing page, clockwise from top left: A tribal woman. A *sadhu* puffs at his *chillum*. Agricultural labourers at work in a paddy field. Sikh men performing the *bhangra*, a vigorous dance accompanied by rhythmic drumming and singing.

land of
many faiths

A multitude of faiths exist side-by-side in India, shaping the country's heritage, life and culture. Devotion to worship and a religious way of life (within the framework of a secular state) is a defining feature of Indian society.

f OUR OF THE WORLD'S MAJOR FAITHS meet on Indian soil – Buddhism, Hinduism, Islam and Christianity. The first two took root in India, as did Jainism and Sikhism. India also has significant though small communities of Jews and Parsis or Zoroastrians. Hinduism, which originated as far back as 1500 BC, is the dominant faith with a following of nearly 600 million. Eclectic by nature, Hinduism is the only major religion with no single founder or holy book as the scriptural authority. The Hindu pantheon of gods centres on the trinity of Brahma (the Creator), Vishnu (the Preserver) and Shiva (the Destroyer).

Arab traders brought Islam to India as early as the 7th century, after which various Muslim invaders made sporadic raids into India until,

at the end of the 12th century, the first Muslim kingdom was established. The first phase of Islamic rule in India was aggressive. However, the mystics of Islam, called *sufis*, played an important role in later years by spreading the message of universal love. Today, Muslims form the second largest religious community in India, numbering over 150 million.

Buddhism was an Indian religion for many years before it became a pan-Asian one. The Buddha was born in India, and lived and died here. Buddhists constitute a very small proportion of the population, but the influence of Buddhism can still be seen.

Sikhism, founded in the 15th century by Guru Nanak, is opposed to the caste system and idol worship, and considers the *Granth Sahib*, or the holy book, to be the symbol of god. Concentrated in the north of India, the Sikhs are a recognizable group with their turbans and beards.

India has a 30-million-strong Christian community, belonging to various Protestant denominations and Roman Catholicism. Christianity first came to India through the work of missionaries.

A small Jewish community centred in Kerala and around Mumbai, and Parsis along the coasts of Gujarat and Maharashtra, are among the other religious groups in India.

Facing page: Jain novitiates at the Dilwara temple in Mount Abu, Rajasthan.
Clockwise from right:
God Shiva is widely represented by the *lingam*, a phallic symbol. Here, a devotee meditates before Shaivite *lingams*. Statue of Buddhist goddess Tara, in a monastery in Ladakh. The feet of the Buddha are worshipped in Bodhgaya. Muslims in prayer at the Jami Masjid in Ahmedabad on the occasion of Id.

new delhi
the capital city

Delhi was founded, according to legend, around 1500 BC, as Indraprastha. Successive ruling dynasties chose it as the seat of power.

Facing page, top: The Lotus Temple of the Bahai faith – one of Delhi's most visited sites.

Facing page, bottom: Lutyens and Baker were commissioned to build the city of New Delhi. Their most famous edifice is Rashtrapati Bhavan, the residence of the President of India.

Right: High-rises in India's capital city.

Middle: Raj Ghat, the memorial to Mahatma Gandhi. His last words, "Hey Ram", are inscribed on the granite.

Bottom: Jantar Mantar, the observatory built in 1724 by Sawai Jai Singh of Jaipur.

SPRAWLING ON THE BANKS of the river Yamuna, Delhi, the capital of India, is replete with a sense of history. It flourished more than 3,000 years ago and monuments dating back to the 11th century can still be found around the city and its outskirts. Delhi is also a modern city that reflects the legacy of British rule. The division between Old and New Delhi is that between the capitals of the Mughals and the British who ruled India between the 16th and early quarter of the 18th century.

Above: Gates leading into Rashtrapati Bhavan, the residence of the Indian President, with the four lions, the symbol of the Republic.
Right: Republic Day celebrations in Delhi.
Below: India Gate, built to commemorate the Indian and British soldiers who died in World War I.
Facing page: The historic Qutb Minar in south Delhi – where Qutbuddin Aibak laid the foundation of the Delhi Sultanate in 1193.

the monumental splendours of agra

Agra was the imperial capital of the Mughal court during the 16th and 17th centuries before it was shifted to Delhi.

Far left: The tombs of Shah Jahan and Mumtaz Mahal – these are replicas of the real tombs, which are in the crypt.
Left: Local women at the Taj, their colourful clothes a contrast to the pristine white marble.
Below: The Taj is flanked by two identical sandstone buildings. The one on the left is a mosque, the one on the right was built to maintain the symmetry.
Facing page: The Taj Mahal, India's most famous monument, built by the Mughal emperor in memory of his beloved wife Mumtaz Mahal.

$\mathbb{A}$GRA, LIKE DELHI, lies on the right bank of the river Yamuna, and is closely associated with the Mughal period in Indian history which reached its zenith between 1556 and 1658 under successive rulers like Akbar, Shah Jahan and Jehangir. The Taj Mahal, which was Shah Jahan's memorial to his wife Mumtaz, is synonymous not only with Agra but with India as a whole. It is not just the Taj but the immense range of architecture as reflected in Fatehpur Sikri, Sikandra, Agra Fort, Itmad-ud-Daulah and other monuments, and the handicrafts and traditional jewellery of the city, that bring a steady stream of visitors to Agra throughout the year.

Clockwise from top: *Qawwali* singers at the tomb of Salim Chishti – a revered *sufi* saint – in Fatehpur Sikri.
A Hindu feeds the holy cow in the sacred city of Mathura, near Agra.
The gateway to Itmad-ud-Daulah's tomb, often described as "a jewel-box in marble".
Intricate inlay of marble on red sandstone – Sikandra.
Facing page, top: The sandstone ramparts of Agra Fort crescent along the Yamuna riverfront.
Facing page, bottom: The Diwan-i-Khas at the abandoned Mughal capital of Fatehpur Sikri – a fine blend of Hindu and Islamic architectural styles.

legendary rajasthan
"land of the kings"

Rajasthan houses some of India's most popular tourist destinations. Its singularly beautiful landscape, ornamental palaces and colourful people lend it an exotic quality that is rarely matched.

Facing page, top: The handsome visage of a Rajput – the bright turban is typical headwear in this region.
Facing page, bottom: Mehrangarh fort at Jodhpur.
Left: *Dandiya* dancers of Rajasthan.
Below: The Hawa Mahal or Palace of Winds, through whose perforated screens women watched ceremonial processions.

r AJASTHAN, or the land of kings, is best known for its massive forts and palaces strewn across the desert state. It is home to the Rajputs, a warrior clan that controlled western India for nearly 1,000 years. They were at constant war with the Arabs, and later with the Sultans of Delhi and the Mughals. Forts and palaces built atop the scraggy hilltops of the Aravalli range provided defensive embattlements against invaders. These were massive structures with ramparts running for several kilometres and splendid interiors embellished with inlays and frescoes that are preserved to this day.

Clockwise from top: Jal Mahal, a lake palace, earlier used as a lodge for duck shoots by Jaipur royalty.
Gaitor – marble cenotaphs of Jaipur royalty are housed in a walled garden.
Albert Hall, built in the Indo-Saracenic style.
A deity is carried in ceremonial procession during the Teej festival.
Facing page, clockwise from top: The City Palace of Udaipur.
Young Rajasthani woman peers from beneath her veil.
Anoop Mahal, the hall of mirrors, at Mehrangarh fort.
Interiors of the Bhand Sagar palace in Bikaner.

The ancient Aravalli range to the northwest of the country separates the fertile Dhundar basin from the flats of the mighty Thar desert, widely regarded as one of the driest places on earth. Further west the remote desert outpost of Jaisalmer, built of a local yellow sandstone that glows in the evening light, is the Golden City. The people of this desert region dress in brightly coloured clothes that set them off against the monochromatic hues of the landscape. The heavy silver anklets of the women and the swaggering moustaches and bulky turbans of the men epitomize India at her most exotic. Decorated *havelis*, exquisitely carved buildings and majestic forts are typical features of this arid land.

J AIPUR, the capital city, was founded in 1727 by Maharaja Jai Singh, who moved his capital from Amber to this site. The city, planned according to the Hindu treatise *Shilpa Sastra*, is a rectangle with roads and avenues running parallel to the sides. In AD 1863, Jaipur was dressed in pink to welcome Prince Albert, consort of Queen Victoria and earned for itself the title of Pink City. Besides housing numerous places of interest, Jaipur is also the base from which to explore the surrounding regions of Ajmer, Pushkar, Shekhawat, Bikaner, Jaisalmer, Jodhpur, Sariska and Bharatpur.

Clockwise from right:
A camel caravan travels along the spectacular sand dunes of Rajasthan's Thar desert. People throng around the victory tower at Chittorgarh fort on a festive occasion. Jaisalmer city, encircled by the massive sandstone bastions of the fort.
Facing page, clockwise from top: A temple complex within the fort at Jaisalmer. Folk singers sing bygone tales of chivalry and romance. Gaily clad Rajasthani women at the Pushkar cattle fair.

Right: The Maharaja of Benaras with the royal family at his Ramnagar palace.
Below: Boats anchored at the *ghats* (steps leading to the river) of the Ganges.

sacred benares
on the banks of the ganges

The Ganges, or the Ganga, is India's most sacred river. Rising in the foothills of the western Himalayas, it runs a course of 2,400 km before it empties out into the Bay of Bengal in the east.

tHE GANGES rises in the foothills of the Himalayas about 160 km from the holy city of Hardwar (literally, "gate to god"). It is joined by the Yamuna at Allahabad, and the meeting of these two rivers with the mythical Saraswati is called the Sangam. The famous festival of Kumbh, which takes place once every 12 years, is held at this confluence.

The Ganges is joined by other tributaries as it passes through Benares (Varanasi), a city with over 1,500 temples where pilgrims throng for the "holy dip" that washes away their sins. To die in Benares is ultimate salvation, according to Hindu precept. Its "burning *ghats*" witness thousands of ritualistic cremations every day.

Top: A Hindu devotee at evening prayer.
Middle: A priest performs *arati* – a ritual of worship – to the temple deity.
Left: Devotees throng the banks of the Ganges for the ritual dip.

Right: Sardula, a mythical lion, towers over a half-kneeling woman in a sculpture at the Kandariya Mahadev shrine.
Below: The Lakshmana temple, part of the western group.
Facing page, left: Amorous couples and female figures are the main subject of the sculptured bands on the temples.
Facing page, right: A statue of Ganesh, the elephant-headed god, son of Shiva.

erotic temples at khajuraho

The temples of Khajuraho represent the culmination of the central Indian style of architecture, which evolved over centuries of experimentation.

KHAJURAHO, a beautiful little village in the state of Madhya Pradesh in central India, is famous for its remarkable temples and exquisite sculptures which are more than 1,000 years old. According to local legend, there were once over 85 temples here, of which only 20 survive today.

The temples are divided into three groups, the western group being the largest and best known. Most of them are Hindu, while a few are dedicated to the Jain faith. At the centre of the western group is the magnificent Kandariya Mahadev temple, which stands 30 m above its plinth. The elegant proportions of this building and its sculptural detailing make it one of the most refined examples of central India's artistic heritage. The oldest temple in the western group is the Chausath Yogini, to the southwest of the Shivsagar tank.

Facing page, top: A meditating figure – one of many characters in scenes that are carved into the walls of the temples.

Facing page, bottom: The quality of locally quarried sandstone lent itself perfectly to intricate carving and delicate workmanship. The colour of the stone varies from a pale buff to brown, and reflects the changing light of the sun.

Above: The Devi Jagadambi temple, the only temple in the complex that is still used for worship.

Right: Divine lovers.

Far right: The artist's skill in creating the jewellery, head-dress and a youthful stance is evident in this sculpture of a Hindu deity.

MUCH OF KHAJURAHO'S APPEAL for the visitor rests on the remarkable erotic sculptures that adorn the sides of the temples. These have been interpreted variously as representing a decadent phase of history which witnessed a fall in moral standards and values, as a visual illustration of the *Kamasutra* – the ancient text on the science of love-making, and as historical evidence of a *tantric* sect that practised esoteric rituals. Whatever the explanation, the sensuous decorativeness, exquisite workmanship and artistic beauty of the sculptures continue to be an undeniable attraction.

magnificent ladakh

Ladakh – literally "the land of many passes" – is a magical and remote place, and is variously described as "the Moonland", "Little Tibet" and even "the last Shangri-la". It is one of the world's last enclaves of Mahayana Buddhism, Ladakh's principal religion for nearly a thousand years.

Ladakh is a vast highland desert lying between the Karakoram and Himalayan ranges in the state of Jammu and Kashmir. In its early history, Ladakh was a feudal kingdom of federated clans ruled from the capital, Leh, by a line of rulers that claimed descent from the kings of Lhasa in Tibet. Present-day Ladakh is divided into two districts, Leh and Kargil. Leh is inhabited predominantly by Buddhists and is therefore a centre of Buddhist culture, although it has a sizeable Muslim population. The Great Himalayan range dominates the western part of Ladakh that borders Himachal Pradesh and the Kashmir valley. The Zanskar valley is part of the western district. Ladakh has some of the world's largest glaciers outside the polar regions, and a huge lake – Pangong Tso – that is 150 km long and 4 km wide at a height of 4,000 m.

Facing page, top: The crocus, from whose stamen saffron is extracted.
Facing page, bottom: Leh Palace, Ladakh.
Top left: A *thangka*, or cloth painting, depicting characters and episodes from the life of the Buddha.
Top right: A scenic view of the Tso-Morir lake, set in the high-altitude desert characteristic of the Tibetan plateau.
Above: Masked *chaam* dancers.

cool hill stations

The hill stations of India, which provide welcome relief from the sweltering heat of the plains, owe their origins to the days of the British Raj.

Right: Mussoorie, at 2,000 m above sea level, is a very popular destination in the north. A famous early resident was Sir George Everest, who gave his name to the world's highest peak.

Middle: Naldehra, in the Shimla region, is famous for its nine-hole golf course.

Below: The Mall at Shimla, which used to be the summer capital of the British Raj.

Facing page, top: Ootacamund, or Ooty – the queen of the southern hill stations – stands at 2,240 m above sea level.

Facing page, bottom: A panoramic view of snow-capped mountains from Kufri, situated 16 km from Shimla.

dOTTED ACROSS THE MOUNTAIN RANGES of
the Indian subcontinent are numerous hill stations,
resorts designed as escapes from the summer heat.
Created by the British towards the end of the 19th
century, the hill stations were normally located
wherever a suitable stretch of hills stood convenient-
ly close to a workaday city or town in the plains.
Colonial-style bungalows on terraced hillsides, toy
trains that puff their way up winding railtracks,
clubs that are the hub of social life, numerous
boarding schools founded by the British for their
children – these are some of the characteristic
markers of these hill resorts across the country.
The hill station continued to be popular even
after the Raj came to an end in 1947 – today it
is a thoroughly Indian institution although it
does not hide its British origins.

Left: An interior of Chapslee Hotel, Shimla.

Below: The charming railway station at Coonoor, the second largest hill station in the Nilgiris after Ooty.

Bottom: Fernhill Palace in Ooty. Recently taken over by the Taj Group of hotels, this was once the summer residence of the Maharaja of Mysore.

Facing page, top: A spectacular view of Ooty, spread out among a number of verdant hills in the Nilgiri range.

Facing page, bottom: The entrance to Chapslee Hotel, Shimla.

bustling mumbai
(bombay)

With 16 million people from all over India wedged into it, Mumbai is the economic powerhouse of the nation, the capital of the Hindi film industry, and the land of opportunity where rags can turn to riches.

MUMBAI is an exciting and vibrant city where dreams are fuelled by energy and determination. It is the commercial capital of India and the traditional base of Indian industry. Skyscrapers and colonial buildings jostle alongside industrial slums and the hustle-bustle of markets in this urban metropolis. The most cosmopolitan of Indian cities, most of Mumbai's expansion in recent years has taken place towards the north, along Juhu beach. Mumbai has the world's largest film industry, known as Bollywood after Hollywood. It is also a major port, symbolized by the Gateway of India that was built to commemorate the royal visit of George V and Queen Mary in 1911 although it was completed only in 1924.

Facing page, top: The Taj Mahal hotel, built by the Parsi industrialist Tata in 1903.
Facing page, bottom: The Gateway of India, built to commemorate the visit of King George V in 1911.
Top left: Named after the Roman goddess of abundance, Flora Fountain was erected in 1869 and stands at the intersection of some of Mumbai's busiest thoroughfares.
Top right: Racehorses at the Mahalaxmi Race Course, named after the Hindu goddess of wealth.
Right: An oversized cinema hoarding dominates the streetscape. An estimated 75,000 Mumbai-ites go to the movies every week.

Above: Churchgate, one of the three imposing entrances to the British fort area. Flora Fountain is in the foreground.

Right: The elephant-headed Hindu god Ganesh is held in great reverence and affection. On the last day of Ganesh Chaturthi, the festival celebrating his birth, giant idols of the god are paraded through the streets in huge processions accompanied by dancers, singers, drummers and performers, while chanting devotees exhort him to come back next year. The idols are finally ceremonially immersed in the sea.

Left: Malvan beach, south of Mumbai.

Below: Marine Drive, or the "Queen's Necklace", so called because of the dramatic curve of its streetlights at night, is one of Mumbai's most popular promenades and sunset-watching spots.

ancient cave temples at ajanta & ellora

Cave architecture reached the peak of complexity and design in the magnificent temples at Ajanta and Ellora. Ranging from tiny monastic cells to colossal, elaborately carved temples, they are remarkable for having been hewn by hand from solid rock.

HE AJANTA CAVES in western India contain 30 rock temples that were excavated and painted by Buddhist monks between 200 BC and AD 600. Regarded as among India's finest art treasures, these depict scenes from the Buddha's life and from Buddhist fables. The caves also contain excellent sculptures, including a statue of the Buddha.

Ellora, about 65 km from Ajanta, has 34 cave temples carved out of the hillside. Of these only 12 are Buddhist in character and even these incorporate Hindu and Jain themes. The Hindu temples are the most impressive, especially the magnificent Kailash temple, which is nearly twice as tall as the Parthenon and occupies twice the area.

Facing page, top: The Indra Sabha, the finest of the Jain temples at Ellora.

Facing page, bottom: Local tourists in an Ellora cave temple.

Top: A 7-m figure of the reclining Buddha, depicting his *parinirvana* (ultimate enlightenment or liberation), in one of the Ajanta caves.

Above left: An Ajanta fresco – these frescoes are in grave danger of obliteration and efforts are being made to preserve them.

Above right: Statues of the meditating Buddha under the Bodhi tree.

Right: An external view of the rock-cut caves at Ellora, which comprise Hindu, Buddhist and Jain temples and monasteries.

idyllic goa

What makes Goa unique is its idyllic charm and laid-back atmosphere – its ambience is a successful blend of Indian and European cultures. The Goans are a hospitable people, and their attitude is in tune with the natural beauty that surrounds them.

Facing page, top: The brightly painted portico of a Goan house.

Facing page, bottom: One of Goa's numerous public buildings that are protected under the aegis of the Archaeological Survey of India.

Left: Se Cathedral, the largest in South Asia, and the seat of the archdiocese of Goa.

Below: South Anjuna beach.

Right: Goa's Siquerim beach.
Bottom: Palm-fringed rice fields in Ponda district.

9OA forms a narrow strip of land on the west coast of India. Its 105-km coastline is mostly fringed by long sandy beaches, which are a major attraction for tourists from all over the world. Goa's seven rivers, navigable throughout the year, flow from the Western Ghats down to the Arabian Sea, along lush, green paddy fields and coconut and cashew plantations. The impact of 450 years of Portuguese rule (from 1510 to 1961) is evident throughout this state. Panaji, the capital, and surrounding towns such as Margoa, Vasco, Mapusa and Pilar boast a number of splendid Christian churches built by the Portuguese. Goan cuisine is famous for its blend of Portuguese and Indian traditions. Goa today has a number of first-class hotels along its beaches with modern facilities to attract the tourist.

Top: Red chillis, an essential ingredient for the Goan *vindaloo*, for sale in a market in Mapusa.
Middle: The altar at Bom Jesus cathedral.
Left: The salon of the Mrs Meneza Braganza mansion, in Chandor.

colourful kerala
a lush, tropical paradise

"God's own country", is how Kerala is best described – myth has it that the goddess Bhadrakali selected this land as the one place on earth where she would reside. Kerala's lush natural beauty contains a storehouse of legend, romance, history, culture and tradition.

Kerala, the smallest state of southern India, is tucked away in the southwestern corner. Being a coastal state, it was open to a number of outside influences in its long history: first from the Arabs, then the Chinese, the Portuguese, the Dutch and the British. The Kerala of today is, therefore, a rich mosaic of ethnic groups and faiths. It is one of India's most beautiful states with an endless patch-work of lush, green paddy fields, high plantations of teak, pepper and rubber, and palm-fringed beaches and waterways. Unique to Kerala are her backwaters. Chinese-style junks and country boats with thatched roofs ply these waters. Kerala is also known as India's festive land. Festivals are marked by great elephant processions, snake-boat races and colourful Kathakali performances.

Facing page: The backwaters of Kerala.
Above: The art of mime reaches its peak in the highly stylized performance of Kathakali with elaborate make-up and colourful costumes.
Left: Country boats are a commonly used means of getting around in this land of numerous waterways.
Below: Bekal fort, on a beach-head high above the sea.

Right: A spectacular display of Pooram festival elephant ornaments.
Below: A mosque at Vizhinjam, a fishing village near Trivandrum.

Above: Possibly developed as military training in the 11th century, Kalaripayattu, a form of the martial arts, is still practised in Kerala. It is marked by training in both self-defence and attack, and uses weapons like swords, shields, spears and daggers.

Left: The Pooram festival in Thrissur is marked by processions of elaborately bedecked elephants carrying priests and deities, to the accompaniment of extraordinary drumming and fireworks.

Below: The Western Ghats in Kerala are an ecologically sensitive zone with dense tropical evergreen forests and a variety of flora and fauna.

the former kingdom of mysore (karnataka)

Karnataka, formerly the kingdom of Mysore, has a fine balance of natural attractions and historic architecture.

K ARNATAKA, where the south and the north of India truly meet, is a state with diverse landscapes, from its coastal belt and northern plains to its dense forests, and is dotted with architectural treasures that are a major draw for the visitor. To the north are impressive relics of a Muslim past – the Golgumbaz in Bijapur and the massive fortress in Bidar. To the south are the magnificent relics of the ancient city of Vijayanagara. The state's well-preserved religious architecture includes the superbly crafted Hoysala and Chalukya temples dating back to the 6th century, and the 10th-century Jain sculpture at Sravanabelagola.

Facing page, top: The majestic Bengal tiger in the Nagarhole wildlife sanctuary.
Facing page, bottom: His Highness Shrikantadatta Narasimharaja Wodeyar, the Maharaja of Mysore, performing a *puja* on the occasion of Dussehra.
Above: Sri Chamundeshwari temple, on Chamundi Hill, Mysore.
Right: The Government Museum in Bangalore, the capital city.

Right: An ascetic doing *suryanamaskar* – saluting the sun in prayer.

Below left: The 18-m-high monolithic statue of Jain saint Gomateshwara, at Sravanabelagola.

Below right: Hidden in a remote, thickly forested corner of the Western Ghats, the Jog Falls drop over sheer red-brown sandstone cliffs from a massive height.

Left: Tank Vithala at Hampi.
Below: A statue of Mahishasura
– goddess Durga is believed
to have slain this demon king
in Mysore.
Bottom: The gardens of Taj
Karavali hotel in Bangalore.

courtly hyderabad
capital of andhra pradesh

An important centre of Islamic culture, Hyderabad is central India's counterpart to the Mughal splendour of the north.

HE TWIN CITY OF HYDERABAD-SECUNDERABAD, the capital of Andhra Pradesh, combines Hindu and Islamic influences. Almost half its population is Muslim and it is unique among the southern cities in that Urdu is the major spoken language. An acute scarcity of water and overcrowding at Golconda, 12 km to the west, led Mohammed Quli of the Qutb Shahi dynasty, to build the new capital of Hyderabad on the banks of the Musi river in 1591. In 1687 Mughal emperor Aurangzeb overthrew the dynasty and appointed Nizam, his former general, as viceroy. This Asaf Jahi dynasty ruled from Hyderabad until 1949. Although rebuilt and modernizing at a fast pace, the city retains some of its old courtly character through its lively bazaars and its legendary *nawabi* cuisine.

Facing page, top: *Ashur khana*, a painted doorway.
Facing page, middle: Painted stone carvings at the Sri Kalahasti temple.
Facing page, bottom: Boats are used to ferry people across the Godavari river which runs through the state of Andhra Pradesh.
Left: The magnificent Golconda Fort, situated on a steep granite hill. It was used by the last of the Qutb kings as a bastion against Mughal attack.
Below: Charminar (literally "four towers"), Hyderabad's most famous landmark. It was built in 1591 to commemorate the end of a local plague.

madras (chennai)
gateway to the south

Chennai, formerly Madras, capital of Tamilnadu,
is the fourth largest city in India.

SITUATED ON THE EAST COAST OF INDIA, Chennai has been a historical destination for sea-farers, spice traders and cloth merchants. It grew into a city from a number of small coastal villages that included its former namesake, Madraspatnam. Some time around AD 58 the apostle Thomas (Doubting Thomas) is said to have arrived in Madras from the western coast of India, and in AD 78 he was speared to death on a small hill there, now known as St Thomas Mount. The city played a major role in British India as the capital of Madras Presidency.

The cultural identity of this region has been shaped by the Dravidians, who were the original inhabitants since at least the 4th millennium BC, and who were probably displaced from the north by the Aryans. Tamil, India's oldest living language, is over 2,000 years old and boasts a literary tradition dating back to before the birth of Christ.

Facing page, top: Alarmel Valli, one of India's best-known exponents of Bharatanatyam, a classical dance form that originated in Tamilnadu.
Facing page, bottom: The shore temple or temple by the sea, at Mahabalipuram, south of Chennai, is a World Heritage Site and very popular with tourists. The sandstone temple with a granite base was built in the 7th century by King Rajasimha of the Pallava dynasty.

Top: A streetside flower seller in Chennai. Flowers, woven into garlands, are an important feature of daily life for the average Tamilian. Flowers are used as personal adornment for the hair, as well as for worshipping the gods.
Left: A view of the colonial-style buildings of the High Court at Chennai.

Right: The precincts of the Sarangapani temple at Kumbakonam.
Below: One of the open-air bas-reliefs that adorns the massive rocks in Mahabalipuram.
Bottom: The *gopurams* of temples in southern India are typically decorated with carvings of celestial and animal figures – the more prosperous among them have gold-plated sections.

Above: A scene from the celebrations of Chitra festival at Madurai – ritual spraying of water on god Vishnu, mounted on a golden horse.

Far left: The Vivekananda Rock at Kanyakumari, the southernmost tip of Tamilnadu, where the two seas meet.

Left: A devotee with pierced cheeks, a form of ritual worship.

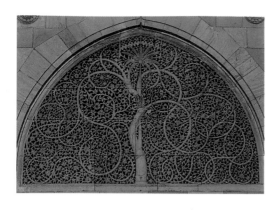

fascinating gujarat

Walled cities, Jain temples, the rare lions of the Gir Reserve and the beaches of Diu make a visit to Gujarat, the birthplace of Mahatma Gandhi, a rewarding experience.

Facing page, top: "Tree of Life" *jaali* at the Siddi Sayyid mosque, Ahmedabad.
Facing page, bottom: View from a height of the Dilwara temple at Mount Abu.
Right: Halvad palace, in the Saurashtra region of Gujarat.
Below left: Porbandar, where Mahatma Gandhi was born.
Below right: Colourfully dressed local women dance the *garba*, a folk form of Gujarat.

9 UJARAT has fascinating and distinctive architecture, a wide variety of scenery and some superb beaches. The state has preserved a rich complex of Jain and Hindu monuments, including the temples at Palitana and Modhera. The cultural capital of the state, Ahmedabad, retains excellent examples of Gujarati provincial architecture. Gujarat also has significant historical associations. Mahatma Gandhi was born in Porbandar and founded his *ashram* at Sabarmati, near Ahmedabad.

Right: Women and children of a semi-nomadic tribe of the Kutch region, wearing their distinctive colourful costumes and elaborate jewellery.

Below: The limestone cliffs of Diu, with its huge fort in the background.

Bottom: The Gir Reserve is the last home of the majestic Asiatic lion.

Facing page, top: A view of the Laxmi Vilas palace in Baroda.

Facing page, bottom: The hill-top complex of Shatrunjaya, one of Jainism's holiest pilgrimage sites, in Palitana.

9UJARAT can be divided into three areas, geographically speaking. The eastern mainland area includes the major cities of Ahmedabad, Surat and Baroda. The Gulf of Cambay divides the mainland strip from the barren Saurashtra region. Gujarat is one of India's wealthier states, with a number of important industries. It is also the former home of a surprisingly large proportion of Indian emigrants, particularly to the UK and USA.

orissa
the picturesque land of temples

Near modern Bhubaneswar, the capital of Orissa, Kalinga was conquered in a bloody battle by the great Indian emperor Ashoka. Shocked at the carnage, he converted to Buddhism and laid the foundations for one of the greatest empires of the world.

Ōrissa is one of the most picturesque regions on the east coast. Its main attractions are the temples of Bhubaneswar, Puri and Konarak, making up the tourist triangle of Orissa, and which draw pilgrims in their millions from across India. Inland Orissa's beautiful hills are home to tribal populations and are one of the most densely forested regions in India. The Buddhist ruins at Ratnagiri, Udaygiri and Lalitgiri dating back to the 5th century AD are well worth a visit. Orissa is also known for its traditions of handicrafts and weaving.

Facing page, top: Surya, the sun god.

Facing page, bottom: The 13th-century Sun temple at Konarak, although in partial ruin, is one of the most vivid architectural treasures of Hindu India, and a World Heritage Site. It is built in the form of a war chariot with 12 pairs of wheels, drawn by seven horses of the sun god Surya. Each of the wheels still functions as a sun dial.

Above left: The Rath Yatra of Puri is an important religious festival. Devotees throng the streets as the main deity of the Jagannath temple is chariot-borne, in ceremonial procession.

Above right: An Odissi dancer, resplendent in costume and jewellery, performs at the annual Konarak dance festival. Odissi, one of the classical dance forms of India, mirrors the postures, expressions and lyrical quality of temple carvings.

Below: Traditional Oriya *nolia*, or fishermen, setting out to sea. Puri boasts a long stretch of golden beaches, dotted with fishing villages.

colonial calcutta
(kolkata)

Calcutta is considered India's intellectual and cultural capital. Rabindranath Tagore, world-famous poet, writer, and India's first Nobel laureate, lived here.

Facing page: Victoria Memorial, a monument to Queen Victoria, was conceived by Lord Curzon as a rival to the Taj Mahal. It was built of white marble from Rajasthan.
Far left: Women dressed in traditional Bengali saris – made of fine white cotton with red borders – immersing an idol of the goddess at the Hooghly river during Durga Puja.
Left: A statue of Lord Curzon at Victoria Memorial.
Below: Taxis lined up outside the busy railway station at Howrah.

iN 1690, Job Charnock, chief of the East India Company, leased some land for new factories from the Mughal emperor Aurangzeb. Six years later, the Company built Fort William, which was rebuilt in its present form in 1773. From then till 1911, when the capital was shifted to New Delhi, Calcutta was the economic, industrial and political capital of India. Today, Calcutta is a bustling commercial hub.

At the centre of the city lies Calcutta's "lung", the Maidan, a vast expanse of land that the British had kept open to give their guns at Fort William a clear line of fire. At the end of the Maidan is the Victoria Memorial, and adjacent to it the imposing St Paul's Cathedral.

CALCUTTA is the second largest city in India, with a population of 14 million. It is a lively city where something is always happening, be it the religious processions during Durga Puja, cricket matches in the famed Eden Gardens stadium, film and theatre festivals, or political demonstrations. The politics of the city is dominated by the Communists who have been democratically elected to govern the state of West Bengal for three successive decades.

Facing page, top left: A stained glass window at St Paul's Cathedral.

Facing page, top right: A roadside fish vendor – fish is a must in a traditional Bengali meal.

Facing page, bottom: An elaborate effigy of goddess Durga in the centre, flanked by goddesses Lakshmi and Saraswati, prepared by local artists during Durga Puja, the most popular festival in Bengal.

Top left: Cricket is a great passion with Calcuttans – Eden Gardens in Calcutta is the largest cricket ground in the world with a capacity of 100,000 spectators.

Above: The hand-pulled rickshaw still provides an inexpensive mode of transport-ation in Calcutta.

Left: Tipu Sultan's mosque, in a busy area of the city.

exotic sikkim

For the people of Sikkim, the Kanchenjunga, or the "Five Treasures of Eternal Snow", is more than the third highest peak in the world; it is the red-robed god who comes riding a snow-white lion to vanquish the forces of evil.

THE MOUNTAINOUS STATE OF SIKKIM is like a
stupendous stairway, leading down from the western
border of the Tibetan plateau to the plains of West
Bengal, a drop of about 5,100 m in 240 km. The
magnificent snow-sheathed Kanchenjunga and the
Tista river, which runs through the state forming a
watershed between Tibet and Nepal, dominate the
landscape of Sikkim, and also the mindscape of its
people. Buddhism is a tangible presence in the state
and its symbols are seen everywhere.

Facing page, top: Young
Sikkimese girl with her school-
bag slung over her head.
Facing page, bottom: The
mighty Kanchenjunga, the
guardian deity of the state,
whose peaks stand over
Sikkim like a palm held up
in perpetual blessing.
Above: Six hundred species of
orchids can be found in Sikkim.
Left: Buddhist school at the
Rumtek monastery.
Below: Buddhist prayer flags
flutter in the wind overlooking
Gangtok, the capital of Sikkim.

curry & spice
the fabulous flavours of india

The Indian "curry", so termed by the British, does little justice to the wide range of temptingly exotic dishes that the different regional cuisines of India have to offer.

Left: Fish wrapped in banana leaves and steamed with a variety of spices.

Below left: Indian meals often end with *kheer* – rice cooked in milk, delicately flavoured with saffron, almonds and decorated with silver leaf.

Facing page, top: The spice box – an essential in any Indian kitchen.

Facing page, bottom: Royal cuisine set out on silver *thalis* – the traditional Indian platter – and served on low tables, makes for a unique dining experience.

Below right: *Makki ki roti* and *sarson ka saag*, served with white unsalted butter – simple rural fare in the Punjab.

Bottom: The *laddoo* – an auspicious Indian sweet – is served at all religious or ceremonial occasions.

INDIA has one of the great culinary traditions in the world. Basically, Indian food is the inspired use of ingredients to bring out in every meal the six main flavours or *rasas* – sweet, sour, salty, bitter, pungent and astringent. Indian food reflects very different cultures and tremendous diversity – from simple vegetarian dishes to elaborate meat, chicken and fish recipes that take all day to prepare.

Each region has its own specialties which are improvised by individual cooks. Restaurants in India range from five-star hotels with specialty cuisines, to open-air fast food places called *dhabas* in north India and *udipis* in the south. Cereals are the staple Indian diet. These consist of *rotis* (unleavened breads) which come in different forms – *paranthas, puris, bhaturas.* Rice can either be served up plain, steamed, or flavoured with ingredients such as spices, meat and vegetables to make delicious *pulaos* and *biryanis.* Most Indians eat with their fingers though visitors are not expected to follow suit.

Above: The ultimate in fine dining and hospitality in the courtyard of Fort Naila, Rajasthan, owned by the Oberoi group.

Right: A tempting display of *idlis* with coconut chutney on a banana leaf – a south Indian delicacy.

Left: Herbs and spices placed on the traditional grinding stone used in Indian cooking.
Far left and below: Indians have a passion for street food, served in a wide range at roadside stalls or small eating places called *dhabas* in the north. These are however best avoided by tourists in spite of their tempting looks.

the amazing crafts of india

The skills of India's craftspeople are legendary, and their products find their way to markets all over the world.

Facing page, bottom: The women in Kutch, Gujarat, start embroidering garments for their dowry from the time they can hold a needle.

Right: A traditional Kalighat painting of the Bengal region – the colonial influence can be seen in the headwear that the men are wearing.

Below: Women of Andhra spin silk yarn which is later dyed and woven into complex patterns to create the famous *ikat* fabric.

Bottom and facing page, top: Silver wire is inlaid onto metal to create a range of Bidri-ware, from boxes to vases.

iNDIA HAS A LONG TRADITION of arts and crafts that has intrigued and awed travellers to the sub-continent throughout history – from the 3rd-century BC Greek traveller Megasthenes, to the 7th-century Chinese pilgrim Hsuan Tsang, Arab travellers of the 13th century like Ibn Battuta, the Europeans of the 17th century, and right on down to present-day tourists. The crafts of India were based originally on the labours of craftspeople at royal courts, and with the loss of this traditional patronage they underwent a decline. However, government support in more recent times has managed to resuscitate some of the most crucial among them. The dexterity of the workers and the elegance of their products, be it in metal, wood, lacquer, textile, paper, stone or terracotta, are undeniable aspects of their attraction.

Right: Ivory and silver bangles are an essential part of a woman's ornaments in Rajasthan.
Far right: A textile block printer at work.
Below: Precious stones set in gold and strung with pearls create a variety of ornaments from noserings to necklaces, anklets and bangles.

e VERY VILLAGE AND TOWN in India boasts
a specialized craft lineage, which is as diverse as
the landscapes, lifestyles and local materials of the
various regions, and which has been passed down
from generation to generation. Lacquer work in
Kashmir, fine shadow-worked embroideries in
Lucknow, painted wooden toys in Andhra and
Tamilnadu, mirror-work embroideries in Gujarat,
tie-dyed fabrics in Rajasthan, brocade weaving in
Benares – the list is endless. India, then, is a veritable
treasure trove of handicrafts and manual skills that
the machine age cannot ever fully obliterate.

Left: A craftsman embroiders with silver and gold thread to create exquisite *zardozi*.
Below left: In Kalamkari painting the fabric is first block printed and then filled in with natural vegetable dyes – this technique was later used to create the exotic chintzes for which the eastern coast of India was famous.
Below right: A Tanjore painting on glass is decorated with gold leaf and semiprecious stones.

an unforgettable passage to india

Indian hospitality is legendary. Wherever you go, you are certain to be made welcome.

NDIA IS ONE OF THE MOST INTERESTING travel destinations in the world. Few other places are home to such complexity, contradictions and natural beauty. It has a history that goes back 5,000 years, traces of which are to be seen in historic monuments and rich artefacts all over the country. Every region of India is different from the others, with its own distinct culture and traditions. Visitors often find it difficult to decide from where to begin.

Facing page, top: The grand Raj Vilas Palace in Jaipur, a favourite destination.
Facing page, bottom: The elegant interior of a train carriage, one of the many ways in which to travel the breadth of India.

Left: Many ancient forts and palaces have been converted to heritage properties – the Samode Palace in Rajasthan, for instance.
Below: Health resorts and spas are fast becoming popular.
Bottom: Luxuriously appointed tents that recall the romance of a bygone era are an exciting alternative to the indoor comforts of hotels.

INDIA CAN OFFER YOU almost anything you want – beaches, forts, temples, tombs, festivals and fairs, music and dance . . . the list is endless. India is not a country, it is often said – it is a continent. Neither is it an easy country to travel around. Yet, for those who have visited it, there is inevitably a hankering to go back. You can never forget nor ignore the colours and contrasts of India.

Above left: A special train that operates tours of Rajasthan – a memorable way to travel.
Above right: A ride on a caparisoned elephant is one of the attractions offered to the traveller at Amber fort.
Right: Samode Palace, a luxurious heritage hotel, surrounded by the Aravalli hills.

Above: A blend of tradition and modernity create a feeling of well-being at a heritage resort.

Far left: Heated indoor swimming pools are offered by most fine hotels in the metropolises of India.

Left: India's vast network of railways includes "toy-trains" which are used to travel to hill stations through picturesque mountainscapes.

Front endpaper: Detail from a mural at Ajanta.
Left: A *sadhu* at Kumbh Mela in Allahabad.

Front cover, top to bottom: The backwaters of Kerala. Shanta Mishra performs the Kuchipudi. The Taj Mahal in Agra.

Back cover, top to bottom: Sri Chamundeshwari temple in Mysore. A *Ramlila* performer. The Maharaja of Benaras with the royal family. Fine cuisine at Fort Naila in Rajasthan.

Published by Periplus Editions (HK) Ltd.

Copyright © 2002 Periplus Editions (HK) Ltd.

ISBN 962-593-852-4

Distributors:

Japan & Korea
Tuttle Publishing
RK Building 2nd Floor
2-13-10 Shimo-Meguro, Meguro-ku
Tokyo 153 0064
Tel: (03) 5437 0171
Fax: (03) 5437 0755

USA, Canada, UK, Europe
Tuttle Publishing
Distribution Center
Airport Industrial Park
364 Innovation Drive
North Clarendon, VT 05759-9436
Tel: (802) 773 8930
Fax: (802) 773 6993

Asia Pacific
Berkeley Books Pte. Ltd.
130 Joo Seng Road
#06-01/03
Olivine Building
Singapore 368357
Tel: (65) 6280 1330
Fax: (65) 6280 6290

Printed in Singapore

Photographic Credits

Arni, Clare, pp. 63 (bottom), 65 (top and bottom right), 70 (top right), 71 (middle right).

Arvidsson, Fredrik, pp. 55 (bottom), 56 (top and bottom), 57 (bottom).

Arya, Aditya, pp. 48 (bottom), 49 (top right), 50 (top), 51 (bottom), 59 (top), 82 (top).

Bagla, Pallava, p. 13 (bottom).

Balan, M., pp. 66 (top, middle and bottom), 67 (top and bottom), 88 (top), 89 (middle and bottom right), 90 (bottom), 91 (bottom left).

Banerjee, Jyoti M., pp. 46 (bottom), 47 (top left).

Bhargava, Subhash, pp. 33 (top), 92 (bottom).

Dilwali, Ashok, pp. 21 (middle right), 39 (right), 45 (bottom), 57 (top), 83 (top right).

East India Hotels, pp. 92 (top), 93 (top right), 95 (bottom left).

Fotomedia, pp. 24 (top), 49 (bottom).

Girota, Phal, pp. 15 (top), 77 (top left).

Gruisen, Joanna van, p. 62 (top).

Khanna, Dinesh, pp. 28 (top, middle right and bottom), 81 (top right).

Khullar, Rupinder, p. 17 (bottom).

Muthuraman, V., back cover (top right), pp. 5, 45 (top), 46 (top), 59 (middle and bottom), 60 (top and bottom), 61 (top, middle and bottom), 62 (bottom), 63 (top), 64 (top and bottom), 65 (top right), 69 (bottom), 71 (top), 81 (bottom), 91 (bottom right).

National Museum, pp. 8 (top left, top right and bottom), 9 (top left, top right and middle), 10 (top and bottom), 11 (top left and top right).

Pasricha, Amit, pp. 23 (bottom), 33 (middle), 44 (middle and bottom), 75 (top), 96.

Pasricha, Avinash, front cover (top left), pp. 6 (top right).

Patankar, Aditya, pp. 6 (middle), 15 (bottom), 32 (middle left and middle right), 34 (top right).

Pfister, Otto, front endpaper, pp. 6 (bottom), 25, 26 (top right), 31 (top), 42 (top and bottom), 43 (top left, top right and bottom), 52 (top), 53 (top, middle left and bottom), 64 (bottom left), 74 (bottom).

Prakash, Dileep, p. 94 (top left).

Ramamrutham, Bharat, p. 51 (top).

Sahai, Kamal, front cover (top right), pp. 6 (top left), 9 (bottom), 11 (bottom), 13 (top left and top right), 26 (bottom), 31 (bottom), 32 (bottom), 33 (bottom left), 39 (left), 40 (top and middle), 41 (top and bottom), 50 (bottom), 54 (top and bottom), 55 (top), 57 (middle), 58, 68 (top), 70 (bottom), 71 (bottom), 79 (top left and bottom), 80 (top left and top right), 81 (top left), 89 (top and bottom left), 94 (top right), 95 (bottom right).

Saith, Sanjeev, p. 37 (bottom).

Samode Palace, p. 94 (bottom).

Saran, Shalini, p. 84 (top).

Satyan, T.S., p. 4 (top left).

Saxena, Sanjay, p. 34 (top left).

Shah, Anal, p. 23 (middle).

Shankar, Sondeep, p. 35 (bottom right).

Sinclair, Toby, front cover (bottom), pp. 16 (top right), 24 (middle), 38 (bottom), 44 (top), 47 (top right and bottom), 73 (top).

Singh, Hashmat, pp. 82 (bottom), 83 (middle and bottom).

Talwar, Amar, title page, pp. 23 (top), 29 (bottom).

Tettoni, Luca Invernizzi (Photobank Singapore), back cover (bottom), p. 86 (top).

Walia, B.P.S., pp. 22 (top), 24 (bottom), 30 (bottom), 49 (top left), 77 (top right), 85 (top, middle left, middle right and bottom), 86 (bottom).

Wilson, Henry, back cover (top left and middle), pp. 7 (top left, top right and bottom), 12 (top and bottom), 14, 15 (middle left and middle right), 16 (top left and bottom), 17 (top left, top right and middle), 18 (top, middle and bottom), 19, 20, 21 (top, left and bottom right), 22 (bottom), 26 (top left), 27, 28 (middle left), 29 (top), 30 (top), 32 (top), 33 (bottom right), 34 (bottom), 35 (top and bottom left), 36 (top and bottom), 37 (top and middle), 38 (top), 40 (bottom), 48 (top), 52 (bottom), 53 (middle right), 68 (bottom), 69 (top), 70 (middle left), 71 (top and bottom), 73 (middle and bottom), 74 (top and middle), 75 (bottom), 76 (top and bottom), 77 (middle), 78, 79 (top right), 80 (bottom), 84 (bottom), 87 (top left, top right and bottom), 88 (bottom), 90 (top left and top right), 91 (top), 93 (top left and bottom), 95 (top).

Discover
exciting asia

Discover Asia with the *Exciting Asia* series. Each title is a visual guide to a different Asian destination. The stunning images within provide a fascinating introduction to each unique and special place. Learn about the country's people and lifestyle, their art and their culture.

New

EXCITING
philippines
a visual journey

Exciting Philippines

text by Elizabeth V. Reyes
photography by Luca Invernizzi Tettoni, et al

A visual splendour of this beautiful country, revealing the uniquely exotic style of its people.

ISBN 962 593 745 5
64 pages Hardcover

Periplus Editions
Each Book: 225 x 300mm
US$16.95 Hardcover
US$9.95 Paperback

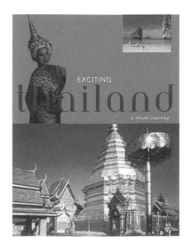

Exciting Bali

text by Patrick R. Booz
photography by Ian Lloyd

An unforgettable insight into the lush Indonesian "Island of the Gods".

ISBN 962 593 210 0
64 pages Paperback

Exciting Malaysia

text by S.L. Wong
photography by Arthur Teng, et al

A visual journey around a fascinating and diverse Southeast Asian nation.

ISBN 962 593 755 2
48 pages Hardcover

Exciting Singapore

text by David Blocksidge
photography by Ingo Jezierski, et al

Feast your eyes on the attractions of this prosperous island-republic.

ISBN 962 593 207 0
64 pages Hardcover

Exciting Thailand

text by Andrew Forbes
photography by Luca Invernizzi Tettoni

An amazing encounter with Thailand's remarkable people and places.

ISBN 962 593 211 9
64 pages Hardcover